101

to

CUT YOUR TAX

101 WAYS
to
CUT YOUR TAX

by

GRAHAM M. KITCHEN, F.C.A.

Edited by Michael Bailey

**Consultant: Annie Bailey, A.C.A., A.T.I.I.
of Moores Rowland Chartered Accountants**

foulsham

LONDON · NEW YORK · TORONTO · SYDNEY

foulsham

Yeovil Road, Slough, Berkshire SL1 4JH

ISBN 0-572-01670-0

Copyright © 1991 G. M. Kitchen

Printed in Great Britain at St. Edmundsbury Press, Bury St. Edmunds.
Photoset in Great Britain by Typesetting Solutions, Slough, Berks.

CONTENTS

Problem Area: BABIES, CHILDREN, STUDENTS AND GRANDCHILDREN

Maternity pay; child care facilities; one parent families; how students can avoid paying tax; education grants; gifts to children.

(1) Question

I left my job recently to take maternity leave and I have been receiving statutory maternity pay from my employer.

Much to my surprise, he is deducting tax. Is this correct?

Answer

Yes, I am afraid it is. Maternity pay is considered to be taxable in the same way as sick pay, etc.

However, if your total income for the tax year (6 April to 5 April) is less than your personal allowances, or if you pay too much tax, then you can claim tax back by asking your tax office for a tax return to complete.

Advice

Remember, that if you plan to return to work for your employer, there is a strict timetable by which you must formally advise him, in writing, of your intention to return to work. If you miss the due date, you could risk losing your rights to your old job back.

(2) Question

I have recently returned to work after the birth of our baby son.

I use the services of a child minder to look after him whilst I am at work. Am I correct in saying I can claim the cost of the child minder as a taxable deduction from my salary?

Answer

Regretfully not. Many people have misunderstood the child care provisions, for the scope for tax relief is in fact very limited.

Employees can only benefit from the use of child care facilities if they are *provided by their employer* if:

(a) the child is under 18

(b) the premises are not domestic premises

(c) the premises are provided by the employer (or a group of employers or a local authority) with each employer(s) being responsible for finance and management

(d) the facility is paid for directly by the employer (in other words, cash allowances, vouchers or reimbursement would not qualify).

If the above conditions do not apply, then you will pay tax on the value of the benefit provided.

(3) Question

We are a one-parent family. Can we get an extra tax allowance?

Answer

Yes — claim the *additional* personal allowance when you fill in your tax return. You can claim this every year for which your child is living with you and is under 16 at the start of the tax year or, if older, is receiving full time education, or on a training course for at least two years.

You can also claim the allowance for a child under 18 who is not your child but who is living with and maintained by you.

An unmarried couple living together as man and wife can only claim one additional personal allowance between them.

Advice

Leaflet IR92 is available from your tax office free of charge and this gives more detailed advice.

In addition, of course, there may be social security benefits you can claim from your local Department of Social Security.

(4) Question

Our daughter, who is at college, has a holiday job two or three times a year, but her employer is deducting PAYE tax even though her earnings in a full year will be less than the personal tax allowance. How can she avoid having tax deducted?

Answer

It sounds as if your daughter has not yet been issued with a PAYE code. An employer has to deduct PAYE at the basic rate until an employee can produce a code.

Your daughter should ask her employer for form P38(S). This, when completed and handed back to the employer, will enable payment to be made without tax deductions.

If the period of work straddles the tax year end (5 April), the Easter holidays, for example, two forms P38(S) will need to be completed.

Advice

If you have been unable to get your tax sorted out by the end of the tax year (5 April) and you have had tax deducted, ask your local tax office for a tax return, fill it in and ask for a repayment of any tax overpaid.

(5) Question

My son receives an educational grant from the local authority towards his polytechnic expenses.

Do either of us have to declare this 'income' for tax purposes?

Answer

No, such a benefit is tax free.

Advice

If your son obtains a holiday job, the grant does not have to be included in your son's total income before reaching the tax threshold.

⑥ Question

We would like to give our recently born grand-daughter some money so that it can be invested for her benefit later in life.

Is there a tax efficient way of doing this?

Answer

Your grand-daughter became a taxpayer in her own right from the day she was born, and therefore is entitled to her own personal allowance, and the annual capital gains tax exemption limit.

The investment you choose is up to you — a unit trust is probably ideal. The investment would have to be in the name of one of the parents, but with a stipulation on the paperwork that it is for the benefit of your grandchild.

Advice

It would be advisable, when you hand over the money, to give a letter to the grandchild's parents confirming that the investment is a gift to be marked for her sole benefit. This would avoid any complication at a later date if the origin of the monies becomes blurred by time and the tax office should one day perhaps think the monies came from the parents. (In that event, the income would be declarable on the parents' income tax return if the amount is over £100 a year.)

⑦ Question

Can either my husband or I transfer any assets to our children without incurring a tax liability on any income from these assets?

Answer

The only way in which parents can transfer assets to their children without continuing to pay tax on the income from those assets is by setting up an irrevocable trust which can accumulate income until the child is 18. If income *is* paid direct to the child before then, it will be taxed as the income of the parent, if the amount exceeds £100 a year.

Problem Area: HUSBANDS AND WIVES

The best time to get married; transfer of married couple's allowance; independent taxation — who is liable; joint bank account to save tax.

(8) Question

I plan to get married sometime next year. Is there a best time for tax purposes?

Answer

In the year of marriage a husband can start claiming the married couple's allowance — but it is reduced by one twelfth for each complete month that he remains a bachelor between 6 April and the month of marriage.

Therefore, the earlier you get married in the tax year (say April, May or June) the better — purely from a tax point of view.

(9) Question

In spite of equal opportunities, the husband still legally gets the married couple's allowance. Can it be transferred to his wife if it is tax advantageous to do this?

Answer

Yes, but only if the husband's income is at such a low level that he is not able to fully use all of the married couple's allowance. It can then be transferred to his wife, if she has sufficient income to make full use of it. Write to your tax office asking for Form 575.

Additionally, in certain circumstances, the husband's personal allowance can also be transferred to his wife if he is unable to use all, or part, of it but there are complicated rules governing this. Ask your tax office for leaflet IR82.

(Conversely, it is not possible for the wife's personal allowance to be transferred to her husband. If she has insufficient income to use this allowance, then it is lost.)

⑩ Question

As a married woman I have just sent in my tax return — the first one I have completed since the introduction of independent taxation.

If I find I am unable to pay the tax demand based on my return, can the tax office insist that my husband pays it?

Answer

No, the tax office can only legally demand any tax due from you and consequently can issue a summons against you and against any assets that you personally possess, including your share of any assets held jointly with your husband (e.g. your house).

Advice

If you see such a situation developing and it is not one that could be resolved by discussing it with your husband, then it could help if you go and talk, confidentially, to the tax office — they may be sympathetic and allow you time to pay.

⑪ Question

Is it possible to transfer our joint bank account into my wife's name only, and set the gross interest against her personal allowance? She has no other income, and her personal allowance would otherwise be lost.

Answer

Yes. You *can* make a such a transfer, but bear in mind that once you effectively gift the money over to her then it will legally become her property *absolutely* to do with it whatever she wishes.

Problem Area: **DIVORCE OR SEPARATION**

What to do when you separate; how to apportion allowances; maintenance payments; insurance policies as a protection.

(12) Question

We have recently separated. Do we need to tell our tax offices?

Answer

Yes. Both a husband and wife should write to their respective tax offices which will be either the office covering their employer's PAYE district, or their local tax office. The tax office can then alter PAYE codes, where applicable, to adjust personal allowances, or send a form to complete if either of you want to claim tax relief for maintenance payments (see question 14).

(13) Question

My wife and I have recently separated. How do we apportion tax allowances?

Answer

In the year of permanent separation, you can claim the full married couple's allowance for that tax year, although it *can* be transferred to your wife (at your option) if your income is insufficient to use it all.

In addition to the normal personal allowance to which each individual is entitled, your wife can claim the *additional* personal allowance if your child is living with her, and the child is under 16 or, if older, is receiving full-time education, or on a training course (including YTS) for at least two years.

Advice

The additional personal allowance is also given for a child under 18 who is not your child but who is living with and maintained by an adult. (Ask your tax office for leaflet IR92 — "A guide for one-parent families" — which gives more background information.)

(14) Question

As part of our divorce arrangements, my wife's solicitors are negotiating with me to consider making maintenance payments. Do I get any tax relief?

Answer

You cannot get tax relief for UK maintenance payments unless there is a legal obligation to make them, for example under a separation deed or court order. Such payments must be made for your wife's maintenance, or for the maintenance by her of any of your children under the age of 21.

Tax relief is not available if your ex-wife remarries, nor is it available if you make payments direct to your child.

You must pay the maintenance gross, that is without deducting tax, and you get tax relief, up to a maximum equal to the married couple's allowance, by either having your PAYE code amended, or by getting an adjustment to your tax assessment.

Advice

Maintenance payments can include periodical cash payments and any bills you pay on behalf of your ex-wife, provided such payments are under a court order, or are legally enforceable.

(15) Question

Under a Court Order made last year, I receive maintenance payments from my ex-husband. Do I have to declare them on my tax return?

Answer

Yes. It is advisable to do so, but you will not be taxed on the amount of the maintenance payments.

Advice

There are special rules for maintenance payments made under a legally binding agreement made before 15 March 1988 or a court order applied for on or before that date, but in place by 30 June 1988. Ask your tax office for leaflet IR93. In certain circumstances you can benefit by making an election to transfer to the current tax relief levels.

(16) Question

I am getting divorced, and it has been suggested by my solicitor that I take out an insurance on my husband. Why is this beneficial?

Answer

If your husband is to provide regular payments as part of a divorce settlement (for example, paying the mortgage on the house in which you are living), these could stop should he die, or have to give up work, say through ill health. To have an insurance based on his life could provide cover for this contingency.

Advice

It is important, for tax purposes, that such insurance is set up in the correct way and you would be well advised not only to consult an independent financial adviser, but have it double-checked by a solicitor.

Problem Area: PAYE QUERIES AND TAX CODES

How does an employer know how much tax to deduct?; how to check your tax code.

(17) Question

PAYE tax is deducted from my salary, but how does my employer know how much to deduct?

Answer

Your tax office will have given your employer a code which tells him your total tax free allowances before tax is calculated.

You should have had a *coding notice* from the Inspector of Taxes which gives you the details. If you haven't received this, write to your tax office and ask for one.

Your employer will be able to tell you what code he is using, but he would not have any details as to how it is made up as that is confidential to you.

At the end of each tax year (5 April) every employer, by law, has to give every employee a Form P60 which shows your total earnings for the year and the amount of tax deducted (or refunded). You should check this to see that you haven't paid too much tax.

Advice

When you get your P60 form, it is important to check that the tax you have paid is correct, for if it is wrong, your code is probably incorrect; if that is the case, it is also likely that your previous year's tax may also have been wrong.

You can go back six years if you feel you have made a mistake. Write to your tax office and ask them for a tax assessment for each year. If it is found that you have overpaid tax, you will get a refund.

(18) Question

When the personal allowances are altered in the March Budget each year, how are they able to take effect by

6 April if the employer's tax tables have already been printed and distributed?

Answer

The tax office sends out a circular to each employer, usually in early May, directing most PAYE codes to be altered to reflect any changes made in the personal allowances and married couple's allowance in the Budget, and back-dating them to 6 April. Keep a look out to see that your tax is reduced slightly.

Advice

Always check the P60 form that you get from your employer at the end of each tax year to make sure you haven't paid too much tax. It is surprising how many employers forget to make these code alterations.

(19) Question

How can I check whether my PAYE code is correct?

Answer

You should have received a Notice of Coding from your tax office. (Ask them for a copy if you haven't had one.) Even if you do not have this to hand, you can check your code as follows:

Add together all of the following:

Allowable expenses

Retirement annuity relief (for personal pension plans taken out before 1 July 1988).

Personal tax allowances to which you are entitled (e.g. personal allowance, married couple's allowance, additional personal allowance).

Personal pensions where you are a higher rate taxpayer and you have received tax relief by deducting your pension contributions from your salary.

Maintenance payments.

Mortgage interest paid gross and not having had tax deducted under the MIRAS scheme.

Covenants to charities, if you are a higher rate tax payer entitled to further tax relief (for the basic rate tax will have been deducted from the payment).

Then deduct from this total any of the following items that are applicable:

   Pensions (including the State retirement pension).

   Benefits (e.g. car benefit, fuel benefit).

   Taxable expense allowances.

   Casual earnings, commissions etc.

   Income from property.

   Interest received gross.

   Unemployment benefit adjustment (see question 27).

   Maintenance payments (see question 14).

This net total is the figure on which your code is based.

In fact, the tax office omit the last digit to arrive at your code. For example, if the net total is 3,500 your code would be 350. (This means you can earn £3,500 of taxable income before you start paying tax.)

As well as a code *number*, there will be a *letter*. This defines your status for tax purposes (e.g. single, married, pensioner). This enables your employer to adjust your code quickly if allowances change in each year's Budget.

Advice

A recent survey showed that at least 20 per cent of PAYE codes are wrong. Checking your code now could save you tax.

Problem Area: **BENEFITS AND EXPENSES**

How to reduce benefits from company cars; what expenses you can claim if you are on **PAYE**; working from home; car parking; money or benefits-in-kind; home expenses.

⑳ **Question**

As part of my remuneration package I get a company car — at present a Vauxhall Cavalier 2500cc.

Is there any way I can get a reduction in the amount of car benefit and private fuel benefit on which I currently pay tax?

Answer

If you do at least 18,000 miles on business travel in a year, you can claim a deduction of 50 per cent on both the car benefit and private fuel benefit.

Your employer should have declared this on a Form P11D which he has to send to the tax office in April each year, but you also have to give the information in your tax return.

Advice

Do you really need a car with such a high cc? If you change it for a car that is under 2000cc your taxable benefits will reduce by over a third!

If you are unable to use a company car for a period of at least 30 consecutive days (for example, you are abroad, or have an accident) then the car benefit is reduced proportionately if you declare this fact in your tax return.

㉑ **Question**

I have a company car and my business mileage is only around 6,000 miles a year. I am being taxed on this benefit using the official scale charge. I accept that the car benefit charge is fair, but do I have to pay the full private fuel benefit?

Answer

You may be able to reduce the fuel benefit. Calculate how much petrol you use just on private mileage. If you reimburse your employer this amount you can avoid being charged the private fuel benefit altogether — compare the amounts involved, however, for it may be to your advantage to accept the *scale* charge if the tax on this is less than your private mileage fuel bills.

Advice

Mileage from home to your permanent place of business is generally considered by the tax office as *personal* mileage, so take this into account in doing your calculations.

(22) Question

I work for an employer and pay tax under PAYE. Are there any expenses I should consider claiming, or does the fact that I'm on PAYE prevent me from claiming any expenses?

Answer

The fact that you are taxed under PAYE does not automatically mean that you cannot claim expenses, it is just a little more difficult to convince the tax office. For you to claim expenses against earnings you have to pass the tax office test; is the expenditure wholly, exclusively and necessarily incurred in carrying out your job? If the answer is 'yes', then provided the expense is not reimbursed by your employer you could claim such expenditure on your tax return.

Factory and manual workers might consider claiming overalls or other protective clothing (and the cost of cleaning) if they are necessary for their work and provided at their expense. Similarly with tools, trade journals or technical books.

Sales managers, or representatives and office and clerical staff, might pay fees or subscriptions to professional bodies, or use their private telephone from home for office work — they could claim a proportion. If you use your home as an office, consider claiming a proportion of the expenses (see question 25).

Advice

You should detail in your tax return your claim for such expenditure. It is often helpful if you can get a letter from your employer confirming that while your expenses are justified and necessary for your job, they are not reimbursed as a matter of policy. Attach such a letter to your tax return.

(23) Question

I work in a city centre and fortunately my employer allows me a free parking space.
Is this taxable as a benefit?

Answer

It would have been prior to 5 April 1988, but the tax law changed from that date to make such a perk free of tax.

(24) Question

My employer has offered me a choice of either a salary increase, or a TV and video for use at home.
In terms of money value they are the same, but are there any tax advantages?

Answer

It is usually beneficial to take a benefit (or perk) rather than a salary increase for, provided it is not specifically stipulated in your contract of employment, you will not pay national insurance on the benefits.

From a tax point of view, if your earnings (and benefits) are less than £8,500 per year and you are not a director, the loan of the asset will be tax free. If you are a director, or earn more than £8,500 p.a. you will be taxed at 20 per cent of the market value.

Advice

You must declare such a benefit in your tax return.

Remember, the employer must *buy* the asset for you — if you are given the money to buy it yourself, you will pay tax and national insurance on the cash payment as part of your salary.

(25) Question

My employer expects me to work from my home on occasions. Can I claim any expenses for so doing and will I run the risk of having to pay capital gains tax when I eventually sell my house?

Answer

If you find you have to do additional work for your employer in your own time, and use a room in your home, you ought to claim an allowance based on a proportion of the total upkeep of the room, e.g. rent, light, heat, insurance, cleaning, repairs to furniture, etc.

Claim the expense when you fill in your tax return.

If you use a room in your home *wholly* for doing your employer's work, then you do run the risk of being charged capital gains tax when you sell the house. Such tax liability would be based on the proportion that the area of the room bears to the total number of rooms.

Problem Area: UNEMPLOYED

Transfer of tax allowances; unemployment benefit; compensation for loss of office.

(26) Question

My husband has been unemployed for several months. I have a full time job myself, but can I claim any of the tax allowances which my husband cannot use?

Answer

Yes. You can certainly ask the tax office to transfer any of your husband's unused married couple's allowance against your earnings. (Ask your tax office for claim Form 575). If you are paying allowable mortgage interest, and again your husband's income is insufficient to take full advantage of the tax relief, you can ask for the relief to be utilised against your income. (Ask your tax office for Form 15.)

Finally, there are a limited number of circumstances where any unused portion of a husband's personal allowance can be transferred — leaflet IR82 available from your tax office will help here.

(27) Question

I have been receiving unemployment benefit for several months and I am confused by the amount of tax that is being deducted by the Department of Employment.

What is the position?

Answer

Each person's unemployment benefit is assessed by a 'benefit officer' at your local Department of Employment office who decides how much tax to deduct.

The amount of tax deducted will depend on your personal circumstances. Generally speaking, the officer will try and gauge your tax liability so that you neither overpay nor underpay tax for the year.

At the end of the tax year (or period of unemployment)

the officer will assess your tax position and make any repayments of tax to you if too much tax has been deducted. Your tax inspector will also be told.

Advice

If you restart work, then at the end of the tax year (5 April) check your total income, less allowances, to make sure you haven't paid too much tax. Often there is a delay in your new employer applying your correct PAYE code and you may be due a refund (see question 19).

(28) Question

I would like to leave my current employment and I have been led to believe from my employer that I would be given £10,000 (equivalent to six months' salary) were I to leave amicably.

Will I have to pay tax on this?

Answer

The first £30,000 of compensation for loss of office, payment in lieu of notice, or ex gratia payments (including redundancy pay, incidentally) is free of tax *provided* such compensation is not stated as a right under your contract of employment.

Advice

Your employer should give you a letter stating that such sum *is* in lieu of notice (or whatever) so that you have some evidence in case it's challenged by your tax office.

What to do if your tax office doesn't reply to letters; late tax returns.

(29) Question

I have written several times to my local tax office and can get no satisfactory answer to the queries on my tax return. Is there anyone else in the Inland Revenue to whom I can turn for advice?

Answer

Write to your District Inspector — the address will be in the telephone directory under 'Inland Revenue'. Mark the letter 'Complaint' and state your problem and the fact that your local tax office will not respond. Be sure to state your tax reference number and national insurance number.

If no help is forthcoming, write to the Regional Controller — again the address will be in the telephone directory, or ring the tax enquiry centre listed for your area.

Advice

Whilst it is often necessary to write a letter to the tax office, the whole tax system revolves around 'forms'! It is often quicker to get a response to a tax query by either filling in a tax return, or asking for a tax assessment. Your problems will often be dealt with more quickly if you fill in the correct form rather than sending in a long rambling letter.

The tax office also have available leaflet IR52 which gives further guidance.

(30) Question

I don't usually send in my tax return for several months after 6 April. Does it matter?

Answer

Yes, it does. The Inland Revenue have tightened up

considerably of late. Legally, your tax return should be sent in within 30 days from the date of issue. Even if you cannot complete all the sections in the return, still send it in, making it clear that other information is to follow.

If you do not send in your tax return by the due date, you could be involved in penalties and interest payments. Such interest is at a compound rate and is not allowed as a tax deduction.

If you are on PAYE, your code could also be wrong, resulting in your paying too much tax.

Problem Area: **TAX ASSESSMENTS AND REPAYMENTS**

How to check and respond to tax assessments; how to claim tax repayments.

(31) Question

I have received a tax assessment from my tax office for benefits that they say I have received from my employer. On querying the figures, the Inspector states that they refer to sums declared by my employer on a P11D form. The 'benefit' is made up of car benefit and fuel benefit (on which I have no disagreement), and a huge sum for travelling, subsistence and entertaining. What is a P11D form, and how should I respond?

Answer

All employees whose earnings, expenses *and potential benefits* are at the rate of £8,500 a year or more, and most directors', regardless of their earnings or expenses, have their benefits and expenses reported to the tax office by their employer. The employer has to do this by law and fills in the notoriously complicated form P11D which is sent to the tax office.

Your main query seems to revolve around the assessment for expenses and, on the assumption that all this expenditure was made on behalf of your employer in the course of your work and reimbursed by him, and that such expenditure was solely spent on the business of your employer, then you should send a letter to your tax office stating that fact.

The tax office may want further details to ensure that you derived no personal benefit — which of course *would* be taxable.

Advice

In future years ask your employer for a copy of the P11D form if you can, then include in your own tax return a claim for the allowable business expenditure to be offset and this should prevent assessments arising in the future with this type of problem.

You should attach a letter to your tax return stating that the expenditure was "wholly, exclusively and necessarily incurred on the business of your employer", if such was the case.

(32) Question

I have received a tax assessment from my tax office saying I owe them £150 from two years ago.

As I could not understand the calculations, I didn't do anything about it, and now I have had a final demand.

Do I have to pay?

Answer

Probably you will have to pay.

There is a 30 day limit for appealing against an assessment and as you did nothing to challenge the amount assessed or to ask for help in getting it explained, then the collector of taxes is in his right to demand the money.

A sympathetic letter to your tax office might help. Alternatively, if you haven't sent in a tax return for the last two or three years then it might be a good idea to complete one. In checking the tax return the tax office might discover that *they* were wrong in making the assessment and you might be able to claim back the £150. It might be worth a try.

(33) Question

I pay tax under PAYE and I have received a notice of assessment from the tax inspector. Please explain this, and indicate how I can, and should, respond.

Answer

The tax inspector sends out a notice of assessment either because:

(a) you have asked for one in order to check your tax, particularly if you think a tax repayment is due to you.

(b) the tax office has discovered that there has been an overpayment, or significant underpayment, of tax.

If you agree with the assessment and you have underpaid tax, this will normally be carried forward and recouped by the tax office in the next year by a change in your PAYE code — a notice of coding will be issued identifying the change. If the tax office consider it impractical to collect any underpayment in this way (for example, your taxable benefits may exceed your allowances for next year), then you will receive a tax demand for the sum due.

In the case of an assessment showing an overpayment of tax, a refund will normally be made to you.

If you disagree with the figures, then write to the tax office explaining your reasons. Do this within 30 days of the date of assessment otherwise, if you do not, you will get a tax demand for the amount underpaid.

If you do not agree the tax payable, always write to the Inspector of Taxes, never the Collector of Taxes.

Ask any tax office for leaflet IR37 for reference.

(34) Question

What is the quickest way to claim a repayment of tax?

Answer

Ask your tax office for leaflet IR112. This not only gives you advice but has at the back a Form 95(D) "Request for a repayment claim form" which you should complete and send to your local tax office. Ensure that you state your national insurance number.

Repayment claim forms are normally used by people who have received income which has had tax deducted, but because they have no other income, or have a fairly low income, then they do not reach the tax threshold and are able to claim tax back. Such people would normally be pensioners, married women not in employment or in part-time employment, and children under 16.

Normally a repayment form should be sent to your tax office at the end of each tax year (5 April) but if the amount overpaid regularly exceeds £50 then you may be able to get more frequent tax repayments.

Advice

Remember to include with your Form 95(D) any dividend vouchers, or other documentation, verifying that tax has been deducted.

(35) Question

I have just realised that I haven't been claiming back the tax deducted from dividends over the past few years. How far can I go back?

Answer

Claims for repayment of income tax must be made within a period of six years from the 5 April of the year to which it relates.

Write to your tax office asking for a tax return for each year, complete them and when returning them ask for a repayment to be made, stating your reasons.

Problem Area: MISCELLANEOUS TAX QUERIES

Commission earnings; working abroad; private health insurance; national insurance; VAT; football pools winnings.

(36) Question

I am a married woman and I earn commission from part-time selling, and as a catalogue agent.
What is my tax position?

Answer

You can earn up to the amount of the personal allowance without having to pay tax. For amounts over that sum you should declare your earnings in a tax return and you will have to pay tax on the excess over the personal allowance. Commission earned on your own purchases from your catalogue is not taxable and should be excluded from your calculation.

Bear in mind, however, that you might be able to claim expenses against such income, for example cost of travelling to customers' houses, stationery and postage, and any other expenditure "wholly, exclusively and necessarily" (this is the tax office's definition) spent on carrying out your business.

Advice

Do not consider avoiding declaring such income if it is above the taxable limit — remember that most companies have to make an annual declaration of such payments to their tax office so that the tax inspector can do some spot checks.

(37) Question

I have been working in Europe for an overseas company on and off now for the past few years on the understanding that my earnings are all tax free. Is this correct, and do I have to declare them in my tax return?

Answer

If you are absent for 365 days or more, then all your earnings from that employment are free of UK tax. You can, however, return to the UK for incidental duties and holidays within certain limits. Intervening days you spend in the UK must not exceed 62 consecutive days, or one-sixth of the total of those days and the number of days in each of the qualifying periods you spent outside the UK *immediately* before and after the UK visit.

If you receive a pension as a result of overseas employment, you will normally get a 10 per cent deduction, but more relief may be available under any double tax agreement between the country concerned and the UK.

Advice

If you have a company car in the UK on which you are taxed as a benefit in kind, claim a reduction in the benefit for that proportion of time you were unable to use the car because you were abroad for a period of at least 30 consecutive days.

(38) Question

My father-in-law is over 60 years of age and cannot afford to keep paying private health insurance premiums. If I pay them on his behalf can I get any tax benefit?

Answer

Yes, provided both you and your father-in-law are resident in the UK. This would apply to any relative. Anyone paying private medical insurance for themselves, or their husband or wife, can also get tax relief on private medical insurance payments provided they, or one of the couple, are over 60 years of age.

Advice

You get basic rate tax relief by deducting tax from the premium when you pay the insurance company. If you are a higher rate tax payer, then you can claim the excess in your PAYE coding, or tax assessment, at the end of the tax year.

(39) Question

Is there any way of reducing the amount of national insurance that my employer deducts from my salary?

Answer

There are two options you could consider:

(a) Contracting-out of the Government State pension scheme, and taking out a personal pension plan. This would reduce your national insurance contributions, and could give you a better investment for the future. Very broadly speaking, it is beneficial to do this if you are under 40 years of age (30 for a woman) but contact an independent financial adviser to get the facts before doing anything.

(b) When negotiating your next pay rise, you could ask your employer to give you a benefit-in-kind instead.

Most benefits escape the national insurance charge.

(40) Question

My wife is disabled and we have spent a considerable sum in adapting our bathroom to make life easier for her. Can I get any tax relief for this expenditure?

Answer

Unfortunately not. Neither can you get any tax relief on any interest paid on borrowed money as it is classed as a home improvement and not allowed for tax.

Advice

You do not have to pay VAT on the cost of the alterations, so if VAT has been charged, omit it from the invoice. If you have already paid the sum, write to your local Customs & Excise VAT office (the address is in the telephone directory) and ask for a form to claim a refund. You will need to produce the receipted invoices as evidence.

(41) Question

I have just won some money on the football pools and a friend tells me that I should declare my winnings on my tax return.

Is this right?

Answer

Your friend is quite wrong. All winnings from gambling by a private individual are tax free and don't have to be declared to the tax office.

Problem Area: HOUSES AND MORTGAGES

How much mortgage interest can you get allowed for tax, and what you should tell the tax office; bridging loans; MIRAS schemes; joint mortgages; home improvements.

(42) Question

What is 'allowable' mortgage interest, and how do I claim tax relief on it?

Answer

Interest is allowed for basic rate tax relief on total loans not exceeding £30,000 if the loan is for the purchase of a main residence of the borrower, or land on which to build one, in the UK or Republic of Ireland.

There is no relief on the interest on the amount of the loan *over* £30,000, nor is there relief for overdraft interest. Interest is also allowed for tax on loans taken out *prior* to 6 April 1988 if the loan was to *improve* a house.

When you take out your mortgage, the lender will give you a MIRAS certificate which you send to your tax office. This will enable you to deduct tax from the interest element at the basic rate when you make repayments.

There are also special rules concerning dependant relatives and marriage separation.

(43) Question

We purchased our new house, which is our main residence, some months ago with the aid of a bridging loan from the bank. However, we still have not been able to sell our original house.

With higher rate tax relief having been abolished on allowable mortgage interest we really are finding it financially difficult, for we effectively have lost out on the higher rate tax relief on both mortgages. Is there anything we can do?

Answer

There were special provisions announced in the March

1991 Budget to help people in just the same situation in which you find yourselves.

You will only lose the higher rate tax relief on the bridging loan; you will still get the higher rate relief on your original mortgage (up to the £30,000 limit) provided the bridging loan was either made prior to 6 April 1991 or, if made after that date, must have been in respect of a binding contract made prior to 6 April 1991. Your tax office will also want to see proof that the loan offer was made before that date.

(44) Question

My wife and I are taking out a £20,000 mortgage to buy our own home, and plan in a year or two to increase this to finance improvements when we feel more able to cope with the repayments. Are there any tax pitfalls?

Answer

Yes. Even though you are not borrowing the full amount on which you can get allowable mortgage interest, when you top up your mortgage this will be classified as a home improvement loan and the interest on this additional loan will not qualify for tax relief.

Explore all avenues (in particular, low cost mortgages) and get a bigger mortgage initially if you can, in order to take full advantage of the tax benefits.

(45) Question

I rent out a flat that I own and have a mortgage on the property. Can I claim tax relief on the interest, and does the £30,000 limit apply?

Answer

On the assumption that you do not live in the flat yourself, such a property is likely to be regarded as an investment property by the tax office. Interest will be allowed, but only if the property is let at a commercial rent for at least six months in each year and available for letting, unless being repaired. The £30,000 limit does not apply, and you can claim interest against the letting income. If the interest paid exceeds the rental income then the excess can be carried forward to the following year.

Advice

As an investment property, you should consider claiming expenses against any letting income to reduce your tax liability. Consider claiming:

Water rates.

General maintenance and repairs of the property, garden and furniture and fittings.

Costs of agents for letting and collecting rents.

Insurance.

Charges for preparing inventories.

Legal fees — on renewing a tenancy agreement, for leases of not more than 50 years, or on the initial grant of a lease not exceeding 21 years.

Accountancy fees to prepare and agree your property income.

Costs of collecting rents, which could include your travelling expenses to and from the property.

Costs of services, e.g. porters, cleaners, security.

Wear and tear allowance for furniture and fittings, generally 10 per cent of the rent receivable. As an alternative, the cost of renewals may be claimed.

Note that the community charge (poll tax) will not be allowed as a deduction unless it is levied at the standard rate on the property.

(46) Question

We have recently had an extension built on our house, and I am told that as it is a home improvement I can claim back the VAT that my builder has charged on his invoices. Is this correct?

Answer

Unfortunately you cannot claim back the VAT. Neither, incidentally, can you get any tax relief on a loan for home improvements.

Advice

Make sure your builder is *registered* for VAT. There are a number of jobbing builders around who charge VAT but who are not registered and therefore have no legal right to charge VAT — they are merely pocketing the VAT element for themselves and not passing it on to Customs and Excise. If the builder is registered he should have a VAT number quoted on his invoice to you which you can check with your local Customs and Excise branch if you have any doubt.

(47) Question

Am I right in saying that allowable mortgage interest on our main residence can be allocated between my wife and I in any way we choose, regardless of who actually pays the mortgage repayments?

Answer

Yes, this has been the case since 6 April 1990. When you send in your tax return, ask your tax office for Form 15 and this will enable you to tell them how you want the interest apportioned.

It should be beneficial to consider apportioning mortgage interest relief in the following circumstances:

(a) if the loan is outside the "Miras" rules, ensure the person liable to tax claims the tax relief — you will get no benefit if you are not liable for tax at all.

(b) if you are aged 65 or over, allocate the interest to avoid the age allowance earnings restriction.

Advice

You must send Form 15 to your tax office *within twelve months* after the end of the tax year in which you want it to apply.

(48) Question

I am not married but have purchased a house to live in, together with three friends, who also share the mortgage.

Does the £30,000 limit for tax interest relief apply to each of us?

Answer

The £30,000 limit applies to the *property* regardless of the number of borrowers. It *is* possible for several residents each to have a mortgage on the same house, but the total loan must not exceed £30,000 for tax interest relief. The maximum relief each owner of a property can have will be "£30,000 divided by the number of borrowers". If an owner is not utilising his or her full portion, the difference can be transferred to another owner of the same property for tax relief purposes.

Problem Area: GIVING TO CHARITY

Tax efficient ways of giving to charity; how to get tax relief; giving shares to charity.

(49) Question

I am a taxpayer and I want to give regularly to charity. Obviously I would like to take advantage of any tax concessions. What options should I consider?

Answer

There are three main ways of giving to charity in a tax efficient manner:

(a) Payroll giving schemes:

Persuade your employer to start one of these schemes whereby you agree to pay a monthly (or weekly) sum to a charity.

The donation is deducted from your pay and passed on to the charity by the employer. PAYE is calculated on your salary *after* making the deduction so that you are effectively getting tax relief on the donation at your highest tax rate.

(b) Gift Aid:

A scheme whereby a *single* gift can be made to a charity net of basic rate tax so that the charity can claim repayment of the tax.

Higher rate tax relief is also available to the giver by claiming the payment in their tax return.

(c) Covenant:

A deed of covenant is a legally binding agreement and to be effective for tax relief must be for a minimum of three years. You get this relief by deducting tax at the basic rate from the payment. If you are a higher rate tax payer, any excess can be claimed on your tax return.

For payroll giving schemes there is a maximum amount that is allowable for tax and there is a minimum amount in the case of Gift Aid. The amounts are usually amended in each year's Budget.

Advice

Obviously in all cases you must be a tax payer in the first instance to benefit — if you don't pay tax these schemes are not tax efficient (see question 50).

(50) Question

I am a married woman and pay a monthly sum under a deed of covenant to a registered charity. How do I get tax relief?

Answer

You effectively get the tax relief by deducting tax at the basic rate from the payment to the charity when you make the deed of covenant; for example, if the basic rate of tax was 25%, then if you paid £15, it is worth £20 to the charity. You can claim the higher rate relief in your tax returns, if appropriate (see below).

Advice

If your total income does not cover your personal allowance so that you are not liable to tax you cannot legally get tax relief on a deed of covenant, and the tax office will ask you at the end of the tax year to repay the tax that you have deducted.

With the introduction of independent taxation in April 1990 under which all wives are treated as individuals in their own right for tax purposes, getting their own tax return, being responsible for their own tax affairs and getting their own individual tax allowances and exemptions, it was important for married women to review their deeds of covenant. Many have not done so.

To overcome the problem, either cancel the deed of covenant and have it reissued in your husband's name (assuming he is a taxpayer) or see if you can allocate your tax affairs, perhaps by transferring interest-bearing savings into your name so your personal allowance is not wasted.

(51) Question

I plan to sell some shares on which I am making a profit

and give the proceeds to a charity. Is there a tax efficient way of doing this?

Answer

Yes. You will benefit if you arrange with a stockbroker or bank to transfer the shares themselves directly to the charity concerned. This way your gift will be exempt from capital gains tax.

If you sell the shares first and then make a cash donation, the shares could be liable to capital gains tax if you have exceeded your annual capital gains tax free limit.

(52) Question

I have taken out a deed of covenant to a local registered charity and deduct tax at the basic rate.

My total income is such that I am in the higher rate tax bracket. Can I get extra tax relief?

Answer

Yes. Although you can only deduct basic rate tax when you make the payment to the charity, at the end of the year (after 5 April), when you should fill in your tax return, there is a section in the return in which you can give details of the deed of covenant.

In calculating any tax under or over paid your tax office will allow the deed of covenant as an allowable expense at your higher rate of tax, and this will be taken into account in either making a tax repayment to you, or lessening any underpayment of tax.

Pension scheme options; contracting out of SERPS; transfer values.

(53) **Question**

Can you explain why pension schemes are such a tax efficient investment?

Answer

There are three main reasons:

(a) The tax inspector effectively pays part towards your pension as the contributions are allowable for tax at your top income tax rate.

There are limits over which tax relief is not available and these vary from year to year.

(b) A pension scheme will provide you with additional income to supplement your State pension when you retire.

(c) A tax free capital sum can be taken on retirement.

Advice

In calculating the maximum pensions limit that is tax allowable, benefits in kind can be included in total income.

(54) **Question**

It would be helpful to have a short explanation of the main pension scheme opportunities so that I can invest any surplus income to best advantage.

Answer

There are basically four main ways in which you can contribute to a pension scheme:

(i) An **employer's scheme**, whereby either you or your employer, or both of you, contribute to the scheme. Any contribution you make will be deducted from your salary before PAYE is calculated, and this is how you will get your tax relief. There are maximum limits for tax relief.

(ii) **Additional Voluntary Contributions** (AVCs) — these are top up sums over and above your agreed contribution that you can pay independently of your employer's scheme and you obtain tax relief as above.

(iii) **Free-Standing Additional Voluntary Contributions** (FSAVC) — instead of topping up extra sums to your employer's scheme, you can pay into a separate scheme and you would deduct tax at the basic rate before paying the premiums; if you are on higher rate tax, any additional relief would be claimed on your tax return.

(iv) **Personal pension plans**
If you are self-employed, or not a member of an employer's pension scheme, you can get tax relief on the payments made to a personal pension plan. You can have more than one personal pension plan. There are maximum limits for tax relief related to a percentage of earnings (or profits if you are self-employed) — but the maximum increases over certain ages — 36 and over for personal pension plans, and 51 and over for retirement annuity premiums. These maximum figures are often increased in each year's Budget.

(55) Question

I took out a personal pension plan over three years ago and contracted out of the State earnings related pensions scheme (SERPS).

Should I have received a national insurance rebate?

Answer

Yes. You will not get the rebate personally, but part of your national insurance contributions should be channelled through to your personal pension fund. You should get an annual statement from your pension company advising you of this rebate.

The volume of people contracting out caused a massive amount of work for the Department of Social Security (DSS) and some pension companies are still receiving monies from the DSS going back a number of years, so be sure to check that your pension plan *is* receiving the rebates.

It is important to ensure that all monies due to you are paid into your pension plan, otherwise it could restrict the amount of pension you can get from the policy when you do eventually retire.

Advice

If your pension company cannot help you (or they are also snowed under with paperwork) write to:

> Personal Pension Group
> Department of Social Security
> Contracted Out Employment Group
> Newcastle-upon-Tyne
> Tyne & Wear
> NE98 1XY

(56) Question

I recently changed jobs and found that the transfer value of my company pension had decreased from the figures quoted to me only a year or so ago. Can transfer values fall as well as increase?

Answer

Yes, values can fluctuate in the short-term because of the vulnerability of investment markets generally. Additionally, a group fund can be affected by such things as the average age of the members fluctuating, thus increasing or decreasing the pension company's risk factor.

The calculation of transfer values of pension schemes can vary enormously.

Advice

Check the scheme's rule book to see if there are any specific rules of calculation and check with at least two independent financial advisers on their opinion of the transfer value quoted. You can sometimes get a revaluation if you challenge your insurance company's calculations, particularly if you have some independent evidence.

(57) **Question**

A colleague in the insurance business tells me that everyone would be better off contracting out of the Government State earnings related pension scheme (SERPS), taking the corresponding national insurance rebate that the government is offering, and investing the money in a personal pension plan to get the tax advantages. Is this correct?

Answer

No, it is certainly not correct to say that *everyone* would be better off. You need to get advice from an independent financial adviser, for each person's circumstances can vary.

As a general rule, however, it might be beneficial to contract out for males aged 40 or under (and 30 for females), as the longer term advantages of putting the rebate, and ongoing premiums, into a personal pension scheme (or your employer's scheme) should be more financially lucrative in the longer term.

Problem Area: RETIREMENT AND PENSIONERS

Higher tax allowances; early retirement; pension estimates; is the State retirement pension taxable?; tax repayments; house annuities; tax liabilities; tax and savings.

(58) Question

My husband is 66 next birthday. Can he claim a higher tax allowance?

Answer

Yes. Everyone is entitled to the basic personal allowance and from 6 April of the tax year in which your husband reaches the age of 65, he will be able to claim a higher level of personal allowance. The married couple's allowance is also at a slightly higher level once a husband (or a wife, if older) reaches this age band. (Both allowances increase even further when the age of 75 is reached.) There is a section in the tax return covering pensions, in which you can claim these higher allowances.

Advice

Make sure you have allocated income from any savings and investments to ensure that both you and your husband use your allowances to the full.

The higher personal allowance will be reduced if your income exceeds certain limits.

(59) Question

I am thinking of taking early retirement this year, at the age of 50. How will my pension rights be affected?

Answer

You cannot start receiving the State pension until you reach the age of 65 for a man (60 for a woman). There are, however, no restrictions on your receiving a personal pension earlier if you were in such a scheme, as well as a pension from your company, but this will depend on the rules of the scheme.

Advice

Check with the Department of Social Security to see if you have made sufficient contributions to enable you to eventually draw the full State pension and, possibly, any graduated retirement benefit for contributions made between 6 April 1961 and 5 April 1978. If not, you may need to continue paying voluntary contributions for a while.

(60) Question

I am only 50 years of age at present, but in planning for when I do eventually retire, how can I find out how much I am entitled to under the State pension scheme?

Answer

Write to Department of Social Security, Central Office, Room 37D, Longbenton, Newcastle-upon-Tyne NE98 1YX asking for a retirement pension forecast. You need to quote your national insurance number when making this enquiry.

(61) Question

Do I have to pay tax on my State retirement pension?

Answer

If the State pension is your only income, then it is unlikely you will have to pay any tax as the pension will probably be below your personal allowance.

However, if you have other pensions, or receive any interest or dividends, or have any other form of earnings, then you need to add them all together to find your *total income* for the tax year. From this you must deduct the personal allowances, and any other allowable expenses, and it is on this final figure that your tax liability will be calculated.

Advice

When totalling up your income, any interest or dividends received should be included at the gross amount, that is, the figure before any tax has been deducted.

(62) Question

Apart from my State retirement pension, most of my additional income comes from dividends in stocks and shares. As most of the dividends will have had tax deducted before I receive them, how can I claim a refund of tax?

Answer

At the end of the tax year (5 April) ask your tax office for Form R40 which receives more prompt attention than other requests for repayments. Complete it in the same way as a tax return, and send the form, together with any dividend counterfoils, to your tax inspector.

Advice

As most of your income has already had tax deducted before you receive it, ask your tax office if you can have quarterly or half-yearly repayment claims so that you don't have to wait a whole year to get any tax back.

(63) Question

Now that I am retired, I have very little income, apart from a small pension, but I do own my own house without any mortgage or restrictions. I don't want to move, but on the other hand I do need extra income to make my life easier and happier. What would you advise?

Answer

To improve your standard of living and to increase your spendable income you could mortgage your house to an insurance company and use the lump sum to buy an annuity.

When you receive an annuity payment it consists of two elements — capital and income. The capital portion is non-taxable but the insurance company will deduct tax from the income portion (which you must enter on your tax return) and provide you with a tax deduction certificate, which you may need to claim any tax repayment.

You will not get any tax relief on buying the actual annuity, but provided at least 90 per cent of the lump sum received on mortgaging your house is used to buy the annuity then the interest on a mortgage of up to £30,000 will be tax deductible. You must be 65 or over.

Advice

Annuities are particularly useful if you have no dependents or your children or relatives do not need additional assets.

Bear in mind, however, that any extra income from an annuity could reduce any means-tested social security benefit, could affect your age-related personal allowance and will not take inflation into account in succeeding years. Also you cannot cancel an annuity and get your capital back.

(64) Question

Apart from the State retirement pension, I receive a pension from my former employer from which tax is deducted at basic rate before I receive it. This seems unfair. Can I ask for the pension to be paid gross?

Answer

Probably not. Your tax office will have issued your former employer, or their pension scheme admini-strator, with a code (see question 17) authorising them to deduct tax. Tax offices usually do this with second pensions to ensure that they don't miss out on any tax due and, of course, to avoid having to ask for any tax liability at a later date, which could cause a pensioner financial difficulties or inconvenience.

Advice

At the end of the tax year (5 April) add up *all* your income, including the State pension, and deduct the personal allowance. This net figure is the amount on which you should pay tax at the basic rate. If you have had more than this amount deducted in tax from your second pension, write to your tax office requesting a tax return. Fill it in promptly and return it to them asking for a repayment of tax.

(65) Question

As a pensioner, should I consider a TESSA account?

Answer

A TESSA account can be suitable for pensioners in need of extra income for they can take out net income on a monthly basis if required, and collect the 'tax' element as a bonus at the end of five years.

Provided the capital is not withdrawn, the interest will not have to be declared on the tax return, which means that they are particularly suitable for 65-plus savers who are near to the upper income limit in respect of the age allowance.

Advice

Remember that the interest rates on TESSA accounts are not guaranteed; they can go down as well as up over a five year period. Consider alternatively National Savings Certificates and Income Bonds.

(66) Question

I am taking early retirement at 56 years of age. Will this affect my State retirement pension when I reach 65?

Answer

You need to check with the Department of Social Security office to see if you have been credited with sufficient contributions to guarantee your full pension. If you have not paid enough, then you can continue paying voluntary national insurance contributions to ensure that you get the full State basic pension.

Advice

If, following your retirement, you register as unemployed but available for work, contributions will be credited and, indeed, for unemployed men over 60 contributions are automatically credited without the need to be registered.

Bank and building society interest; Form R85; how to calculate total income for tax purposes; joint accounts.

(67) **Question**

As a married woman I have no other income apart from interest earned on my building society account. Can I get the interest paid without tax deducted?

Answer

You can fill in Form R85, which is available from your building society. (The form is also available from banks, post offices and tax offices). In this form you certify that your income for the year is going to be less than your total tax allowances and once this is lodged with your building society they will pay the interest to you without deducting tax.

Advice

To benefit from Form R85, you must be resident in the UK. This form can also be used for deposits with banks and other financial institutions.

You will need your national insurance number to complete the form correctly. (This is *not* the same number as your Health registration number on your medical card.)

If you do not have your national insurance number then send the form to Inland Revenue, NIN Tracing, Freepost, Bootle L69 9HA. They will trace your national insurance number, fill it in and return the form to you to give to your bank, building society, etc.

(68) **Question**

I sent in Form R85 to my bank earlier in the year as I did not expect to be liable for tax this year. However, I have now started part-time work and my income for the year will exceed my total allowances. What should I do?

Answer

Write immediately to your bank telling them to cancel your registration. They will then revert to deducting tax at the basic rate when the next quarterly interest is calculated.

Advice

It is an offence to complete a Form R85 when you know that your total income for the year is going to exceed your total allowances.

If you deliberately make such a false declaration you can be fined if it is proved that you wilfully tried to defraud the tax authorities. (Obviously the tax office will be lenient on those people who genuinely made a mistake.)

(69) Question

In order for me to decide whether to complete a Form R85 to enable me to get my bank deposit interest paid without tax being deducted, how do I calculate my total taxable income?

Answer

Your total income should include all taxable income you anticipate receiving in a full tax year (that is between 6 April in one year to 5 April in the next). Taxable income would include:

Earnings from all sources.

Most State pensions, other pensions and widow's pensions.

Unemployment benefit (including any income support due to being unemployed).

Sick pay and maternity pay.

Widow's benefits.

Invalidity care allowance and invalidity addition paid with a retirement pension.

Earnings from any job or self-employment.

Interest from banks or building society accounts (the gross amount before tax must be used, not the net amount received).

Dividends and unit trust income (the gross amount).
Rent income and any other income.
Your share of any income from joint accounts.
You do not have to include in your total income calculation:
War widow's pension.
Social security benefits not mentioned above.
Student grants and loans.
If your total income is more than your personal allowance, then you do not qualify to complete a Form R85.

(70) Question

I have a joint bank deposit account with my wife. I am a taxpayer, but she is not. Should we still complete Form R85?

Answer

Unless you have provided the tax office with a declaration to the contrary, it will be assumed that the account is held in equal shares and the interest will be divided equally.

Provided your wife agrees, it should be possible for her to fill in Form R85 in respect of her share only so that she can receive the interest gross.

Problem Area: TAX FREE SAVINGS AND INVESTMENTS

Ways of saving that are completely tax free; saving schemes compared.

(71) Question

I am a taxpayer and I would like to consider ways of saving that are completely tax free, both as regards interest and capital.

Answer

The following eight ideas will provide you with income that is completely tax free as long as you stay within the prescribed investment limits and time limits. Profits are also free of capital gains tax:

   (a) National Savings Bank — ordinary account — up to the first £70 of interest.

   (b) National Savings Certificates, including index linked.

   (c) National Savings Yearly Plan.

   (d) Save As You Earn scheme available from the Department of National Savings, or through a bank or building society.

   (e) Tax-exempt special savings account (TESSA) — available from banks, building societies and many financial institutions.

   (f) Personal pension schemes.

   (g) Personal equity plans (PEP).

   (h) Share incentive schemes operated by your employer.

(72) Question

I am in the higher rate tax bracket and would welcome some ideas for tax efficient savings.

Answer

By far the most tax efficient way is to put as much money as you can each year into a personal pension scheme.

Such contributions are allowed for both basic *and* higher rate tax relief. Any registered independent financial adviser will calculate for you the maximum contribution allowable for tax purposes.

(73) Question

Do I have to declare the interest on my TESSA account to the Inland Revenue?

Answer

You don't have to tell the tax office about TESSA. So long as no more than net interest is withdrawn, it will not have to be declared. However, if you stop your TESSA prematurely, you must declare it.

(74) Question

Both National Savings Certificates and TESSA savings accounts enable a person to earn interest free of tax if the capital is left untouched for five years. Is one form of saving better than another?

Answer

The main difference between the two methods of saving is that you know the rate of interest you are going to get on National Savings Certificates before you purchase them; with a TESSA account, however, although the interest rate may be high to start with, the building society or bank can vary the interest at any time during the five years.

Problem Area: SAVINGS AND INVESTMENTS

Investing overseas; unit trusts; Government securities; life policy redemption; saving schemes.

(75) Question

With the abolition of composite rate tax and with no exchange control in the UK, is it still tax efficient to put my savings into an overseas bank or building society account?

Answer

There is no direct tax saving as all interest has to be declared on your tax return. However, interest from overseas banks and building societies is paid gross (whether you are a tax payer or not) and therefore you do gain a benefit by having the use of that gross interest for, perhaps, several months before declaring the interest in your tax return and being assessed for the tax.

(76) Question

Are Unit Trusts a good investment area, and tax efficient?

Answer

Unit trusts effectively spread your investment over a lot of companies and therefore can fluctuate less than ordinary stocks and shares. Bear in mind that in the short term the value of the units can go down as well as up.

There are no particular tax advantages in a normal unit trust, but since the introduction of personal equity plans there are now unit trusts that are registered as PEP schemes and on which you can effect tax savings.

Under a PEP plan you can invest an annual sum, or a lump sum (each year's Budget announces the maximum sum allowed) the tax benefits of which allow any dividends received, and reinvested interest, to be free of income tax, and any capital gains free of capital gains tax.

(77) Question

I want to buy some Government securities. Do I have to use a stockbroker, or my bank, and are there any tax advantages?

Answer

Provided the securities are listed on the National Savings Stock Register, you can purchase the securities at the Post Office and you will receive interest gross and pay tax later, whereas if you purchase them via a broker or your bank, you will receive the interest net after tax.

The end result will be the same in terms of total tax paid, but your cash flow will be much improved by having the use of gross interest for up to a year before having to hand over the tax.

You can ask at any Post Office for a list of securities covered by this arrangement, and they will also give you an explanatory booklet and an application form.

(78) Question

I have to sell my life endowment policy before the expiry date as I am in urgent need of cash to pay unexpected bills. Are there any tax considerations?

Answer

There are no direct tax savings, but remember that it is often possible to get a loan from the insurance company with whom you have the policy. Provided you keep the policy going, they will advance you a percentage of the value of your policy and use the policy as security. (You will continue to get tax relief on the life premiums by paying them net of basic rate tax if you already receive this relief on your policy.)

Alternatively, instead of just accepting the insurance company's surrender value, you could either sell the policy in the second hand life policy market, or put it up for auction. Higher surrender values are usually obtained by these methods.

Any registered independent financial institution can

give you the name and address of firms that specialise in this sort of business. You will not incur any tax liability on the proceeds of sale, unless the policy did not originally comply with Inland Revenue requirements.

(79) Question

I would like to take out a tax efficient savings scheme that I could use to pay a mortgage and at the same time provide life insurance. I am already a member of my employer's company pension scheme, although the pension is not at a very high level.

What would you advise?

Answer

One of the most tax efficient ways of coping with a mortgage is to take out a pension mortgage. You only have to pay the interest element each year (which is allowed for basic rate tax on loans up to £30,000), the ultimate capital repayment being made from the final pension scheme fund at retirement date before a pension figure is calculated. In addition to the tax relief on the interest paid, you get the pension contribution allowed for tax at your highest tax rate.

As you are already in a pension scheme paid for by your employer, it would be sensible to retain this scheme as it is part of your remuneration package. Ask your employer if it could be used to support a pension mortgage.

Additionally, consider taking out a Free Standing Additional Voluntary Contribution Plan which can be used to increase your pension in retirement. A low cost with-profits endowment plan could additionally provide you with life cover and you could use the policy to fund a mortgage very tax efficiently.

Problem Area: **WILLS, WIDOWS AND WIDOWERS**

The advantages of making a Will; tax reliefs for widows and widowers.

(80) Question

I am married with two children. I haven't made a Will, for in the event of my death I am assuming that our main asset, the house, will pass to my wife.

Is this correct?

Answer

No. Your assumption would be correct if you had no children, but under the laws of intestacy (that is, the laws governing people's property and belongings where there is no Will) your wife will be entitled to all the personal possessions plus £75,000, plus a life interest in one half of the balance of your assets. Your children will take the other half, and take over the house on the death of your wife.

As you will see from this rather simplified example, the house will *not* automatically pass to your wife — she is entitled to "£75,000 worth of it" and therefore if you have no other assets, savings, or investments then, technically, it could be sold in order for the rules of intestacy to apply.

It is a misconception that, on the death of a husband, the family home automatically passes to the wife in the event of no Will having been made.

Advice

It is important to make a Will. It is best to see a solicitor — it doesn't cost much and can take as little as half an hour.

One of the things your solicitor is likely to advise is to put the house into joint names with your wife. Not only will this be helpful in the event of your death, it could also be beneficial if there is an inheritance tax liability.

(81) Question

Following the death of my husband, can I claim any additional tax relief?

Answer

Yes, you can claim the widow's bereavement allowance for the year of death, and one further year.

Surprisingly, a husband cannot claim such an allowance in the event of his wife dying.

Advice

Fill in a tax return and send it to your tax office. There is no specific section on the form enabling you to claim the widow's bereavement allowance, but you are advised to write 'widow's bereavement allowance claimed' under the Allowances section towards the end of the return.

(82) Question

My wife died recently. Am I still entitled to the married couple's allowance for a whole year, or do the Inland Revenue apportion the allowance on a time basis?

Answer

You are entitled to the allowance for the whole year — there is no apportionment.

Problem Area: **CAPITAL GAINS TAX**

How do you calculate the tax rate; indexation allowance; what is tax free; what expenses you can claim.

(83) Question

What is the Capital Gains Tax rate?

Answer

It varies from person to person as capital gains are added on to your total income, less allowances, and taxed at income tax rates — that is either at basic rate or higher rate.

Advice

If you are planning on selling an asset that is going to incur a taxable capital gain and you have earnings that take you into the higher rate tax band, check your past income level to see if you can delay some remuneration until the following tax year in order to have your capital gain taxed at a lower rate.

(84) Question

I have shares which I have held for many years and which have only gone up at about the same rate as inflation.

It seems unfair that when I sell them at a profit I will have to pay capital gains tax when the actual profit is not a profit in 'real terms', taking account of inflation.

Answer

In calculating capital gains tax you *are* allowed to make a deduction for inflation (called an indexation allowance) before calculating any taxable profit.

The tax office have tables that show the inflation rate from month to month.

Advice

As a rough guide, the indexation allowance figure betwen 1982 and 1991 is 63 per cent.

(85) Question

I understand that I don't pay capital gains tax on the sale of my house which I own and occupy and which is my main residence, but can you list other assets on which a profit can be made without having to pay capital gains tax?

Answer

Assets which can be sold free of capital gains tax include the following:

Private motor cars.

Chattels — such as jewellery, pictures and furniture — but there is a maximum limit.

Life policies and deferred annuities.

National Savings Certificates.

Premium Bonds.

Profits on the first sale of shares issued after 18 March 1986 under the Business Expansion Scheme.

Personal Equity Plan (PEP) profits; also transfers of all-employee share schemes to a single company PEP.

Save As You Earn schemes.

TESSA accounts.

Government stocks and public corporation stocks guaranteed by the Government.

Qualifying corporate bonds.

Gambling, pools winnings and prizes.

Decorations for gallantry, unless purchased.

Compensation for damages.

Gifts of assets to a charity.

Gifts of outstanding public interest given to the nation.

Land and buildings given to the National Trust.

Gains up to a maximum limit (set annually) on the sale of your business when you retire.

Foreign currency for personal use.

In addition, each person is allowed an annual exemption limit on all other capital profits (after deducting all or part of any capital losses), and there may be relief for inflation depending on how long you have held the asset (see question 84).

Advice

Remember to offset any capital gains against any losses you have made, or any losses brought forward from previous years.

(86) Question

Can I claim any expenses when I sell an asset and incur a capital gains tax liability?

Answer

Yes. Any expenditure incurred in either buying an asset, or selling an asset, can be claimed when calculating any capital gains tax liability. Any buying expenses should be added to the purchase cost, and any selling costs deducted from the proceeds before calculating any indexation allowance (see question 84).

(87) Question

My husband has made a capital loss in this past tax year on some of his investments whilst I, fortunately, have made a capital profit.

Presumably I can offset his loss against my profit for capital gains purposes?

Answer

Unfortunately not. With the introduction of independent taxation on 6 April 1990, a husband and wife are taxed separately on capital gains and each is entitled to the annual exemption. However, each is accountable individually for any capital losses.

Your husband can carry forward his losses against his future gains and you will have to pay capital gains tax on your capital profits, after claiming any allowable expenses, of course.

Problem Area: INHERITANCE TAX

Who is liable; allocations between married couples; assets that you have inherited or gifted to someone; family businesses.

(88) Question

Is everyone liable to Inheritance Tax, or is it just for the very rich?

Answer

Inheritance Tax is based broadly on the value of a person's assets when they die; in arriving at that value, gifts made by the deceased within the previous seven years may have to be included, although for those made more than three years prior to death any tax liability will be on a sliding scale.

If you own a house, then when you consider the way in which house prices alone have increased over the past ten years or so, it is not surprising how many people will now be liable to inheritance tax.

Not only would you have to value your home at your death, but also any life policy proceeds (but see below), motor car, investments, antiques, silver, stamp collections, etc.

The Budget each year sets a minimum total asset figure under which no inheritance tax is payable.

Advice

If you have a life policy make sure that you identify your husband, wife or children to be the beneficiaries so that the proceeds don't go into your own personal estate.

Also, if you own a house, put it in joint names with your wife.

(89) Question

I am a widower living alone in my own home. My married daughter and her husband are coming to live with me permanently. In order to save eventual capital taxes when I die I plan to transfer the house to them now. Are there any tax complications?

Answer

The transfer will be exempt from capital gains tax as the property is your home. Normally if you gift away your house but continue to live in it, then you cannot escape inheritance tax unless you pay a fair market rent. However, if your daughter and her husband also live in the house and only part of the property is transferred to them, then such a transfer will be exempt from inheritance tax.

Advice

To make such a transfer watertight, it would be wise for everyone to contribute to the running costs of the house.

(90) Question

Two years ago I inherited a house from my father.

As I already have my own home, I will sell my father's. Will I have to pay tax?

Answer

You may be liable to pay capital gains tax, but only on any increase in value (gain) between your father's death (the probate value) and the date of sale. Bear in mind that you can use your annual tax free exemption allowance and claim an indexation allowance (see question 84) before calculating any final tax payable.

(91) Question

My family have owned the business in which I work for many years. I worry that in the event of the death of the major shareholder (my father) the business will have to be broken up to pay inheritance tax.

What should I do?

Answer

Inheritance tax can hit the small family business

particularly hard, whether it is a partnership or limited company.

As your father grows older he should be persuaded to gift part of his holding to other members of the family and you should consider taking out an insurance policy on your father's life to meet any tax payable on his death.

Advice

Get an up-to-date hypothetical valuation on the business from an accountant in order to get any inheritance tax liability in perspective, and know how much life cover to organise.

There are, however, lower inheritance tax rates for small businesses — ask your tax office for leaflet IHT3 which is free of charge and gives a useful background. Also, it is possible to pay any tax due in instalments over 10 years, providing certain conditions are met.

Problem Area: **SELF EMPLOYED**

Setting up as self employed — the best time to start; how to reclaim tax; national insurance matters; pensions; what happens if you make a loss; PAYE problems; how to reduce your tax liability.

(92) Question

I plan to start up my own business in the next few months and be self employed. Is there a best time for me to do this from a tax point of view?

Answer

The date you start is really up to you; it is the date to which you make up your accounts that is important as this will form your accounting period for tax purposes.

You do not have to trade for a full twelve months before preparing your first accounts, so the choice is yours.

Whatever date you choose may not only affect the *amount* of tax you eventually pay but, by choosing a date early in the tax year (say 30 April or 31 May) you can spread any tax payments over a longer period. This is because the tax laws apply a complicated formula for assessing tax in the first three years. Ask your tax office for Form IR105 which will give further information.

Advice

If you have been taxed under PAYE prior to starting business on your own, write to your tax office telling them you are becoming self employed and you may be able to claim back any tax you have paid since the previous 6 April, depending on how much of your allowances have been used.

(93) Question

Having just started in business as self employed, do I have to pay national insurance contributions?

Answer

All self employed people are liable to pay flat rate Class 2 national insurance contributions by buying stamps from a post office or by a standing order through a bank account or Giro.

There is an earnings threshold, so you can get exemption if your income is low, or if you are incapacitated for work.

In addition to paying Class 2 contributions, when you get your tax assessment for the year you may be liable to pay a Class 4 contribution based on your profits. 50 per cent of this Class 4 contribution is allowable for income tax relief in calculating taxable income.

Advice

Towards the end of your accounts year check how much profit you have made — it might be worth putting through extra expenses in the last few weeks, or buying an asset to claim capital allowances, in order to restrict the amount of your Class 4 national insurance assessment.

(94) Question

I employ my wife on a part-time basis in my own business. Are there any ways in which I can limit her tax or national insurance costs?

Answer

If your wife has no other income, then she can earn up to the personal allowance limit before incurring any tax liability.

Note, however, that the level at which national insurance becomes chargeable is at a lower limit than that for income tax. (Check your current national insurance tables to find this limit.)

In order to prevent your wife paying national insurance you could keep her weekly earnings under this limit but pay her a bonus (but still keeping her total earnings under the tax limit) near the end of the tax year, say in March.

That way she (and you, the employer) will only pay a national insurance contribution for the week in which the bonus is paid, giving a significant national insurance saving.

Advice

Note, this will not work if she is a director of your business, for different national insurance rules apply as you are assessed to national insurance on the whole year's earnings.

(95) Question

I am in business on my own and have had a poor year, making fairly low profits. I have purchased machinery during the year on which I can claim capital allowances. Is it beneficial for me to claim these allowances?

Answer

You must first ensure that you are not wasting your personal allowance (and/or the married couple's allowance) for if you have insufficient income to cover your allowances they will be lost. Whereas, if you do not claim capital allowances they *can* be carried forward to future years.

(96) Question

Being self employed, I pay Class 2 national insurance contributions by direct debit as it's easier than going to the post office each week. Are there any disadvantages in doing this?

Answer

The only disadvantage is the fact that as the direct debit is automatic you tend to forget about it; if, therefore, you are sick at any time and are receiving sickness benefit or, perhaps, you are working abroad for a period, you may forget to notify the Department of Social Security of this fact and continue paying the contributions when they may not in fact be due.

(97) Question

I am self employed and employ one assistant. I find the monthly paperwork and payment of PAYE and national insurance very time-consuming. Is there a simpler way?

Answer

If your average monthly PAYE and national insurance is under £400 you can pay quarterly instead of monthly. This will help reduce your paperwork and you can hold onto the money that bit longer to help improve your cash flow!

Advice

Whether you pay monthly or quarterly, always make provision in your budgeting for having to make this payment. A lot of small businesses have been tempted to get behind with payments to the Inland Revenue.

Once you are in arrears it's difficult to catch up, and the tax offices are now very efficient at chasing waverers. They also have preferential claims over other creditors if anything goes wrong.

(98) Question

I have personally borrowed some money in order to go into business in partnership with a friend.

Can I get tax relief on this loan?

Answer

Yes, it will be allowed as a deduction from your income generally (not just the income from the partnership) and should be claimed in your tax return.

Bear in mind that if, previously, you were employed and paid tax under PAYE, then write to your tax office telling them you are going self employed. You may be able to claim back PAYE tax paid in the current tax year, depending on how much of your allowances have been used.

(99) Question

The Inland Revenue are investigating our business accounts generally. How can I get some general advice?

Answer

The best course of action is to ask a professional accountant to help you. It may be expensive, but he will be familiar with the routines adopted by the tax authorities and will advise you on how best to deal with the numerous questions you will doubtless be asked.

Alternatively, the tax office issue two explanatory leaflets which you may find useful. They are IR72 and IR73 available free of charge from any tax office.

(100) Question

I am self employed and as I approach the end of my accounting year (31 March) I can see I have made a good profit. Are there any ways of reducing my tax bill?

Answer

Two ideas should be considered:

(a) If you are likely to buy any cars, plant or machinery in the near future, it would be beneficial to bring forward the purchase prior to your year end. Then, even if you have only legally owned the asset for a few days, or even hours, you can claim a whole year's capital allowance against your taxable profit; (and you can do this even if you haven't yet paid for the asset!).

(b) Consider putting money into a pension scheme. You will get tax relief, and it's better to use the money for this purpose to build a nest egg than pay the money to the tax collector.

Advice

Also bear in mind that if you haven't paid the maximum amount allowed for tax purposes into a pension scheme in previous years, you can 'top up' out of your current year's profits. The rules are complicated, but it's well worth following this through with an independent financial insurance adviser.

(101) Question

I draw £1,500 a month from my own business on account of profits.

Is this the amount on which I pay tax?

Answer

No. Many self employed people think that you pay tax only on what you take out of the business for yourself as "drawings" or "wages". This is not so.

"Drawings" are sums taken on account of the profit you expect to make. You are taxed on your total profit before deducting any drawings.

To find out how much profit you have made, you should prepare an account showing your total business income, less your business expenses. This is not necessarily the figure on which your tax is calculated, however, for you have to add back certain expenses that are not allowed for tax purposes (e.g. expenditure from which you benefit personally — car expenses or personal, as distinct from business, trips are typical examples.) Your own Class 2 national insurance contributions and 50 per cent of your own Class 4 national insurance contribution will be disallowed, as will entertaining expenses and all capital expenditure. In place of capital expenditure, you can claim capital allowances). (Ask your tax office for leaflet IR106.)

It is this amended profit figure, not the one shown in your accounts, that you should enter in your tax return. Your claim for capital allowances must also be entered.

USEFUL ADDRESSES

Banking Ombudsman
Office of the Banking Ombudsman
Citadel House
5-11 Fetter Lane
London EC4A 1BR
Tel: 071-583 1395

Building Society Ombudsman
Grosvenor Gardens House
35-37 Grosvenor Gardens
London SW1 7AW
Tel: 071-931 0044

**Complaints about Independent
Financial Advisers:**

**Financial Intermediaries, Managers &
Brokers Regulatory Assoc (FIMBRA)**
Hertsmere House
London E14 9RW
Tel: 071-538 8860

**The Institute of Chartered
Accountant in England and Wales**
P O Box 433
Chartered Accountants Hall
Moorgate Place
London EC2P 2BJ
Tel: 071-628 7060

**The Institute of Chartered Accountants
in Scotland**
27 Queen Street
Edinburgh EH2 1LA
Tel: 031-225 5673

The Insurance Ombudsman
31 Southampton Row
London WC1B 5HJ
Tel: 071-242 8613

**Occupational Pensions Advisory
Service (OPAS)**
11 Belgrave Road
London SW1V 1RB
Tel: 071-233 8080

Pensions Ombudsman
Office of the Pensions Ombudsman
11 Belgrave Road
London SW1V 1RB
Tel: 071-233 8080

Age Concern England
1268 London Road
London SW16 4ER
Tel: 081-679 8000

Age Concern Northern Ireland
6 Lower Crescent
Belfast
BT7 1NR
Tel: 0232 245729

Age Concern Scotland
54a Fountainbridge
Edinburgh EH3 9PT
Tel: 031-228 5656

Age Concern Wales
4th Floor
1 Cathedral Road
Cardiff CF1 9SD
Tel: 0222 371821
or 371566

**National Council for One Parent
Families**
255 Kentish Town Road
London NW5 2LX
Tel: 071-267 1361

TAX ALLOWANCES

For an up-to-date list of tax allowances:

Write to your local tax office (see Yellow Pages) asking for leaflet IR90.

or

Check the notes with your Tax Return or Notice of Coding.

or

Send a stamped addressed envelope to the publishers of this book, W. Foulsham & Co Ltd, 837 Yeovil Road, Slough, Berks SL1 4JH asking for a tax allowances summary which will be sent free of charge.

For an up-to-date guide on Budget changes each year, with advice on how to fill in your tax return, how to check you are not paying too much tax, how to claim expenses and allowances and general tax advice for everybody including the self employed, buy a copy of CHECK YOUR TAX by G. M. Kitchen and published by W. Foulsham & Co. Ltd.

It is published each year in the month following the Budget.

An Invitation to Write

It is not possible for the author or publisher to correspond with readers regarding their specific queries. However, if you have experienced problems that are not covered in this book, then the publisher would be delighted to hear about them so that the author can include them in the next edition.

PERSONAL REMINDERS

Tax Reference Number ....

Tax Office Address ....

....

....

N.I. Number ....

Tax Returns: Year	Date sent to tax office	Date assessment agreed
....	....	....
....	....	....
....	....	....

Year: ....

Code number checked ☐ ☐ ☐

P60 Form from employer checked ☐ ☐ ☐

Notes on correspondence:

INDEX